Wood Whis

My Woodcarving
By Josef Peeters

Published by Josef Peeters

Author's website:

http://lakesidecaravanpark.wixsite.com/josef

Edited by:

Sarah Farrugia

HEARTT Writing & Editing

cosmo12@bigpond.com / + 61 417 527 123

DEDICATION

I dedicate this book to the person who believes in me, supports me,
and encourages me to explore artistic avenues in any field;
my wife, my friend, and mentor,
Sandy Peeters.

CONTENTS

ACKNOWLEDGMENTS

I commend all the POD and digital platforms available to the Indie author.

1 Beginnings

I have always been cursed with an artistic yearning, yet remained blissfully ignorant of any abilities I may have possessed during my childhood - unable to draw even a stick figure to any degree of satisfaction.

I went on to become a professional actor for a brief period during my twenties, although I had never contemplated treading the boards back in high school. Anything like that would have been considered far too 'uncool' for a young Australian male.

Being vertically challenged with the physique of a toothpick throughout my school years meant that I was too busy fighting for my life, or simply too exhausted from physical and psychological abuse, to attempt anything creative. If I had added anything like drawing or theatre to my repertoire, I probably wouldn't be alive today.

I will admit to having been a closet poet in high school during a period of extreme lunacy, where I didn't care what anyone thought...as long as they didn't know.

My love affair with wood started in my last years of high school, where I started producing quality projects in woodworking classes. Since then, I have been involved with timber almost all of my life in one capacity or another; from selling it, to building furniture for myself. Woodcarving, however, which I explored much later, is a world away from *woodworking*. The two are often mistaken as the same craft – although there can often be elements of each within the other.

My very first attempt at anything resembling woodcarving, came about from necessity when my new partner needed a cane every so often after a bout of Guillane Barre Syndrome, a debilitating auto-immune disease attacking the sheath surrounding the nerves, sometimes leading to partial or total permanent paralysis.

One of our favourite activities is 'sidewalk shopping' as I call it; scrounging around the neighbourhood during hard rubbish collections. I often find a lot of discarded timber that I can 'up-cycle' into a new life – something practical like a coffee table.

On one of my neighbourhood scouting missions, I'd found a likely bit of Cedar that I thought might carve up nicely into a cane. I gave it a shot. Lo and behold, and although very plain, I managed to produce a cane of practical quality. While not demonstrating any degree of artistic flair, I had enjoyed the *process* immeasurably.

At that stage, I did not have the tools required for carving. It hadn't even occurred to me that I might pursue the craft. I wasn't taken with the thought of hacking away at great lumps of wood with chisels and mallets like I had imagined. Carving is all about the removal of excess wood to leave the desired shape. I was not at all keen to venture into that form of tedious labour.

It was not until I attended an agricultural expo where I watched a chainsaw demonstration, that I began thinking about woodcarving with a chainsaw. The idea of removing large portions of wood quickly and easily with a chainsaw appealed greatly to my lazier personality. Two weeks later, I purchased a small second-hand chainsaw and attempted my first in-the-round carving.

Enter, Pig

I immediately saw the nose of a pig in the upturned branch of an improbable lump of wood no doubt destined for somebody's fireplace. The rising distension at the top of the block suggested an ear that poked up comically. It ended up being only half a head, as the log would not allow for a full head with the proportions I had in mind. That led me to discover that one of the most important aspects of woodcarving is in finding the spirit of the wood. 'Listen' to the essence of the wood and it will tell you what it will or won't allow. I did this intuitively at the time. This was reinforced later as I tried to manipulate certain logs into shapes that were not on the wood's agenda. Those pieces are still sitting out in the garden as unfinished, fancy, firewood.

A carving tends to evolve as you proceed, so it pays to 'get with the program'. If you accept and understand this, you get it. Congratulations! If you have no idea what I am talking about, then I suggest you keep an open mind as you read further.

---

1. http://hubpages.com/hub/Carving-4

Many argue that before attempting something new, a lesson or two might be wise. I won't go against such logic if that is something you can afford or wish to do. For me, I prefer to give things a rough shot on my own first. Even now, if there was an opportunity for me to study under a Master Woodcarver I may still gracefully decline. I seem to learn better by 'doing' rather than being taught.

Once you have listened to your piece of wood and accepted that you will work on your carving together, research your subject thoroughly. I cannot stress enough how important pictures and photos are to your work. Make Google your friend, surf the internet, hit the library. It is imperative to have a few pictures of your subject handy at all times throughout your carving process. Referral back to your photos or drawings is essential. I have learned this the hard way.

Our perception changes as the carvings develop, often without our knowledge. Adapt the carving to changing conditions in the wood by all means but never lose sight of your vision and your reference pictures and photos. I have found all too often that overconfidence can produce avoidable disasters.

Researching pigs revealed several good pictures to use as reference material while carving. I then set about readying my equipment. At the time, I had a newly acquired Stihl 009 chainsaw with a sharpened spare chain, chain oil, fuel, and case. Safety equipment should be of good quality and in good condition - earmuffs, goggles, dust mask, and gloves. Dust mask? Absolutely; many kinds of wood have high levels of toxicity when inhaled. Safety chaps are always recommended. I already owned some rudimentary chisels and wood rasps from my woodworking endeavours.

Roughing Out

The chainsaw was powerful (and loud!). It had a 12-inch bar, which proved very efficient. This stage of the carving is commonly known as 'roughing out' or 'blocking' and is the basis upon which, rests the outcome of the carving. I drew a few rough lines on the block where I wanted to cut, then cut outside those lines to allow for further refinement later. It is important not to try to get the exact shape too quickly, getting too close to your outlines, as you will run out of timber when it comes to finishing your piece. Many chainsaw carvers will cut out square blocks for the head, nose, ears etc. later refining the desired features. I do not tend to carve that way as I need to see the shapes emerging early in the piece, to gauge proportions better.

2

At the end of the rough-out, I had to alter my original vision dramatically. Large cracks and voids had appeared in the middle of the log. These were not entirely evident to my untrained eyes at the beginning of the project. My little piggy

2. http://hubpages.com/hub/Carving-4

would have to be a half-head bust with a definite caricature look similar to a Muppet, but I could live with that. It was the wood's desire.

I could see the basic shape I wanted appearing after the initial rough-out. I didn't worry excessively that the overall concept had to change. I had more wood in my pile and did not mind the thought of going through a few pieces to feel out my ability and enthusiasm for the craft.

Timber/wood is not a perfect medium by any means and found wood usually means someone has thrown it out or chopped down a tree for a reason. It could be that the tree was rotten and a danger to persons or property, so it comes as no surprise that found wood has many defects. Even timber purchased from the timber yard can contain defects and voids from sap pockets. I choose not see them as defects unless it renders a carving impossible. I utilise the flaws as much as possible, even emphasising them to great effect in later carvings.

At this stage, a perfectionist would cry out in frustration feeling his brilliant vision was no longer possible. I chose to allow the wood to take me on the journey. As I mentioned earlier, I simply did this intuitively, rather than thinking it through.

After some strokes with a #50 wood rasp, I began to see smoother shapes emerging and found an enduring fondness for this simple tool that allowed me to get up-close and personal with the wood. It remains my favourite hand tool. The wood responded to my manipulations, roundness appeared where once angular, ugly, shapes and ridges protruded. It was highly satisfying. I did not have an angle grinder at the time. If I had, I would have used it in conjunction with a coarse sanding disc and rubber backing pad.

3

Shaping

The next stage is the final shaping of the subject. By this juncture, I was relatively happy with the basic form, but it required details like an eye, a snout, mouth, and more smoothing and shaping of the face in general.

If I had other power tools like rotary tools, grinders etc. I could easily have used them for Pig. I am not by any means a traditionalist who works only with hand tools. I will utilise anything at all that will save my muscles.

At this point, though, saving time wasn't a priority as I was carving for my own experimentation and enjoyment. It is imperative for the professional carver to limit the amount of time spent on each piece. There is no point in working for nothing, or worse, paying someone to take your art. By that I mean, if you charge someone $350 for your carving, but it takes you thirty hours or more, then you are going backward in hourly rates to the point where you are paying the client in your lost time to take the carving off your hands. If you charge as little as $20 per hour and your carving takes 35 hours = $700 to complete, you have lost money. At this price, we've not even taken into account cost of materials such as sandpaper, finishing oils, electricity and so forth. A professional carver

---

3. http://hubpages.com/hub/Carving-4

must consider all these factors when pricing his works, particularly when quoting for a commission.

Pig, was coming along nicely, even though cracks around the top of the head continued to plague my attempts to rescue the carving from its caricature nature. Although I do not mind humorous carvings at all, I was out to define myself with a slightly more dignified piece than a cartoon character. It was not to be. Pig, was coming out of the wood the way the wood decreed and nothing could dissuade it. No amount of corrections, curses or renderings would ever have served to alter the personality of this piece. I had to accept that there were two artists in this project.

Again, I had to go with the flow. I surrendered to a higher authority, proceeding to shape where the wood directed. By now, you probably think I am crackers and you wouldn't be too wrong. I tell you honestly, that once I 'listened' to the wood, everything became a little easier. I did not try to bend the shape to my will anymore; from this point I allowed the wood to take me on the journey.

One thing about carving is that you need tools with rough faces to gain a shape. Unfortunately, if you prefer a smooth finish on your indoor sculpture, you constantly require a finer tool or grit of sandpaper than the last, to wear down the marks left by the previous treatment. The rasp wears down the chainsaw gouges; 40grit sandpaper wears down the rasp marks, 80 grit, 120 grit, 600grit, 1200grit, and leather. It all depends on how far you are willing to go with your piece. There is no right and wrong in the process, there is simply your own creativity leading you to the vision you saw when you first started. Chainsaw carvers often leave their work quite rough, finishing the piece with decking oil because they may be creating outdoor sculptures. I prefer indoor pieces with smooth finishes. Ten different carvers will give you ten different opinions to suit their own personalities and tastes. Everyone is right.

Finishing

After some hours of sanding with an orbital sander with graduating grits of sandpaper, then on to a hand-sanding block for the places the sander could not reach, I was ready for the finishing coats. My piece was by no means a super fine finish to warrant endless coats of oils. I used a couple of coats of Danish oil on Pig, then a coat of natural beeswax.

Traditionally, I do not like paints, clear or otherwise even though I have used them occasionally. During the process of carving Pig, I came upon a personal philosophy with regard to my style of carving. I hold to that philosophy to this day and do not envisage any changes in the future. It is as follows; "I hope to carve a pleasing, recognisable shape, then allow the grandeur of the wood to excite the observer".

I do not attempt to carve highly realistic subjects, preferring a stylised approach with beautiful timber grains and colours shining through the finished product. I love the feel of polished timber. I could cuddle a smooth, polished timber surface for ages without a second thought. When I see someone reaching out to touch one of my woodcarvings, I am ecstatic. It means I have achieved my goal. I have finished that piece to the point where it is irresistible to touch. I like my pieces to invoke a tactile pleasure to my audience as well as being visually pleasing.

It turned out, that while I was working on this carving, my partner was giving a mosaic class to two students, one of whom fell in love with Pig. She purchased him a week later. She wrote to me afterward to tell me how much she loved her, Pig, which resides on her kitchen bench for the entire world to see. She says she adores seeing his happy face when she wakes each morning. "All visitors to her house greatly admire, Pig", she informed me. I take it as a great compliment that I sold my very first in-the-round carving to a mosaic sculpture student whose husband sculpts in aerated concrete. How differently it might have turned out had I given up once I discovered the cracks and voids.

Do you notice the many fissures, holes, and defects in the piece, which I did not try to fill? I learned some very valuable lessons with this first piece. I did not heed all of these lessons every time I carved thereafter, but for each piece, I follow a different journey. Pig was born from Red Gum, a timber most often used for fuel in fireplaces in my country.

I made the transition from hobbyist to an artist with the sale of Pig. Someone reached into their pockets and paid hard-earned cash for one of my carvings. That is the ultimate and final compliment for any artist. The moral is that you should never give up unless everything has failed to the point of no return, and only the carver can decide when that is.

I find that I get to a stage with almost every carving where I hate it and just want to toss it away. Never have I been wholly satisfied with a piece from start to finish.

I love the mesmeric qualities of rasping away at a hunk of wood on my lap. I love the sanding and the finishing. I enjoy the processes, which relax me to the exclusion of all else. Perseverance is the key with almost anything in life, particularly true of artistic endeavour, and never truer than in woodcarving. Everything I wanted to change about, Pig, is what the purchaser loved most of all; the isolated ear, the silly grin, the top of the head that sloped into nothingness. It reminded her of, Piglet, from, Winnie the Pooh.

No one can teach you how to be quirky or original in style. This comes from your personality, while technique and method are relatively easy to pick up if you have the aptitude for learning. I always found learning difficult at school and built up resentment for all things educational. I found I learned easier if I researched topics on my own, at my own pace, and made my own mistakes. I envy persons who can easily assimilate to a schooling environment. I would never have the patience for an education from scratch over many years by a Master, as an apprentice. I simply lack the stamina to endure the process.

When I introduced, Pig, to an online carving community forum, I received comments like, "When I saw, Pig, it made me laugh...", "What a great first carving, it made me smile..." I had produced something special that made people smile. Well, it just doesn't get any better than that.

I began to believe I could be an artist, at last, doing something I enjoyed immensely. I made the transition from hobbyist to serious woodcarver in a very short time. That does not imply that I saw myself as anything other than a beginner with a lot to learn, it simply meant that I had found a passion I wished to pursue with all my heart.

2 Discoveries

I was definitely a beginner, as my next project would prove. I think I made every known mistake in the annals of woodcarving history with my second attempt at carving-in-the-round.

There are quite a few categories of woodcarving, such as; relief, caricature, chainsaw, power, stick & cane, and in-the-round, to name a few. I am fondest of a full, three-dimensional carving with smooth finishes and a certain quality that I believe will make my work stand out. I have seen some outstanding, highly detailed work by Master Woodcarvers that have trained all their lives to master their art. I do not aspire to that kind of perfection. I like seeing someone whose works are original, even though that concept seems almost fanciful these days.

What I hope to achieve with this book is my mindset and thought processes at the time of each carving. I hope to provide inspiration for the burgeoning carver/artist. Basically, I am saying; if I can do it, anyone can. I have posted several works-in-progress threads on the website I mentioned earlier, which gained some notoriety and interest among my fellow carvers. I would like to have expanded my thought processes a little to detail exactly how I came up with an idea, the way I executed it, and the outcome. As with, Pig, I will attempt to guide the reader through a series of stages that resulted in a finished or unfinished piece.

I do not mind admitting to the 'unfinished' projects, which is really just a euphemism for 'failures' by the way. No one should ever expect to be able to achieve all that they desire when working with imperfect mediums and inexperience. I have started several projects where things went awry with proportions causing me to abandon it. We all have to learn as we go along without exception, whether we are learning in a class environment or simply alone in the back yard.

After finishing and selling, Pig, my enthusiasm doubled. I itched to get straight into another carving. The trouble was that my choice of logs was severely limited. Not wanting to spend money on wood when Australia is full of a rich and diverse assortment of native trees limited by options when living in the city of Melbourne. I began to keep a close eye around the neighbourhood to catch any glimpses of felled trees or logs left out on the nature strip for anyone to collect. Jackpot! I found a pile of Yellow Birch logs and limbs. Yellow Birch was to be my favourite timber to carve.

I wanted to carve a Sulphur Crested Cockatoo, indigenous to Australia. I believed I had a suitable lump of wood for the Cocky. Enter my first error in carving, something a professional will point out to any beginner I'm sure.

It is vital to de-bark a log before attempting a carving. The bark may be very thick in some places and super thin elsewhere. It is simply not possible to determine exactly how your vision will eventuate without beginning with a bare log.

The moment I began cutting away, I recognised my folly. I did not take the thickness of the bark into consideration. I did not mind the lean to the left that the carving had taken on, but the proportions were turning out all wrong for the size I had in mind. The first decision I had to make was regarding the crown plumage at rest along the back of the head. Once I removed the bark, too little material remained to carve the shape I desired. I decided to allow the wood to go where it wished by lopping off the plume. The Sulphur Crested Cockatoo would now be a non-descript parrot. Notice my drawings and pictures on the table in the picture below as well as the pencil lines on two faces of the rough carving?

It is necessary to keep adding lines as you go in order to make sure you are still on track with your overall concept. You do not have to be a great artist. I couldn't draw stick figures before I started this venture. The lines will soon disappear. They are merely guidelines for my benefit alone.

Parrot, was born out of the changing proportions of the wood once de-barking took place. I then found problems with the beak. I hit a dead spot- a crack and a small void in the beak region. Once I had eked out of the wood all that it could provide, Parrot no longer had a parrot-like beak, in fact, he began to look something like a Puffin, but the body shape was wrong for me to decide to go that way.

One thing I could not get around was the fact that after debarking the log, it was no longer possible to get accurate body proportions, especially where the wings should have been. At this point, I had to get out of my own head and listen to the wood. I could hear it plainly stating that I should use the disproportionate surfaces to my advantage, make the roughness appearing on the side a part of the design, rather than see them as flaws. I was convinced to disregard realistic appearances for artistic representation. I can hear the professional bird carvers now, wincing as I say this, because their passion lies in total accuracy down to the last feather. My style is about my art being fun, so I stopped worrying about mathematical proportions.

I am not an artistic thinker; that is, I am not a right brain thinker, (Or was that left-brain?). I do not tend to think out of the square at all, or at least, I hadn't to that point. I was always rather conservative in my thoughts and opinions, so this trip into representational art proved as far removed from my personality as possible. My way of thinking was being extended by the wood.

My will was bending to the 'voice' of the wood. I viewed wood in a very different light. What I wanted the piece to be, mattered less and less, as it became increasingly obvious that my initial design contained flaws from the get-go. In retrospect, it turned out to be a very good decision because I ended up gaining two commissions from the resulting carving. My partner's other mosaic student also found my style of carving to her liking, commissioning me to make a cockatoo pendant, then later, a pair of cockatoo earrings. Everything had a reason it seemed.

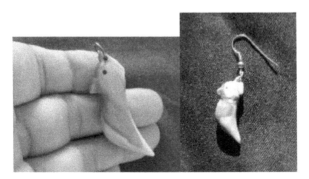

That woodpile of Yellow Birch taught me to listen with my heart and leave the ego behind. I learned within the first few weeks of taking up woodcarving that my journey was to be guided by nature. The wood, urging me to identify myself as a creator with a distinctive style that I could call my own.

I continue to grow as an artist listening to my materials. Prophetically, I carved the two commissions from, 'Parrot', off cuts. At the time of writing this book, I have not sold, Parrot, but I have made money from him none the less. I earned money from my first two woodcarvings, which suggested to me that I might be correct in pursuing this particular addiction.

I refer to wood and timber several times in this narrative. I should explain that wood comes from trees, whereas timber, often used for building purposes, comes from wood. Although it is quite possible to carve from either, timber is generally too small for my carving style. I dabbled for a while with adhering found objects to a basic carved shape before venturing into the realm of pure woodcarving. I have explored several different genres and styles of carving. I am not the ultimate 'wood whisperer' (tongue-in-cheek), by a long shot. I have found many carvers of an ilk to which I can only aspire.

One person, in particular, is Christopher White. His carvings are on a plane of existence far removed from my own ability. Ironically, he is a writer as well, attaching parables and prose to much of his work. After visiting his website, I knew that I was in the presence of artistic genius. His sculptures are sublime, finished to perfection. Were there just one artist to whose works I aspire, it would be Christopher White

I speak of perfection in the context of perception only. His carvings are often incomplete, almost abstract, yet, entirely recognisable. When I say perfection, I mean he has truly seen and heard the wood leading him. He has seen into the soul of the heartwood to extract the very best that the log has to offer. I have seen few others capable of such stunning pieces, with exceptionally glossy finishes painstakingly produced with ever diminishing gradients of sandpaper, finishing with leather at the last. He uses a jeweller's paste to affect his mirror-like surfaces. I have not even scratched the surface when it comes to carving in the manner of Christopher White.

I do not wish to copy him nor mimic his style, but to emulate the same understanding he has with wood. To produce a work from within a log that encompasses the elements desired by both carver and wood. I aspire to be in total harmony with the wood.

For want of a better description, I want to achieve a spiritual alignment between man and nature. The same thing I feel when I walk through a rainforest - trees towering over you, sounds muted and distant, a feeling of comforting isolation. For some, this can be achieved by walking through a cathedral where the spirit is taken to a place of peace and stillness. When I am carving wood, I lose myself to a place devoid of thought, where I am so far 'in the zone' that everything else washes away like a river into the sea. I am at my calmest state of mind when concentrating on a carving or rasping away at a section of the carving, allowing my actions to be free while the rest of me drifts along another path.

For me, woodcarving is the purest form of therapy available. For the cost of a retractable utility knife, you could whittle your way to good mental health in a matter of days, weeks or months depending on your demons. Some carvers are happy to whittle a stick to a point and nothing more. Whatever soothes you is what works for you. It is the journey you take that is the true benefit.

I have an affinity with found wood, including driftwood. I have sold every one of my driftwood carvings - some with no more than a simple eye carved into them. I am sometimes amazed at the number of pieces I have sold considering the short time I have been carving. I have actually been a little embarrassed when selling a couple of my driftwood pieces, as I did nothing more than minute shaping, and some cleaning. It proves the point that I listened closely to the wood to identify the shape it wanted to be and what emerged was attractive enough to warrant a purchase from an admirer.

A ferry ride one glorious day revealed a heap of driftwood washed up onto the banks of the Yarra River. I simply could not get enough of the logs into our tiny vehicle, having driven there after our aquatic sojourn. I was like a child in a lolly shop, seeing all the magnificent shapes emerging from nothing but flotsam and jetsam. I wanted it all.

In one piece, I found a distinctive eye, in another, a stingray waiting to be formed. Everywhere I looked I saw creatures appearing magically from the washed up wood. I could not hear myself think for the voices emanating from the grey, nondescript logs lying about. Some were as soft as butter while others were near petrified, pickled by the brackish water.

I placed the treasure in several piles when I got home: one pile with obvious shapes, another with several possible shapes, and yet another with nothing at all coming to me at the time. Some pieces would need to be left a while to dry out and others I would have to discard altogether as being far too soft. The first piece I chose to work on was the piece with a distinctive eye.

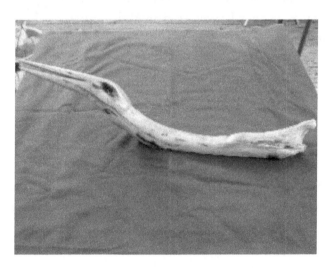

I did not have to do very much to bring, Heron, alive. I shaped the beak with nothing more than a hand saw, flattened a section on the bottom for a base, sanded him smooth, and coated him with clear water-based urethane. I took about half an hour to see him done from start to finish. I sold him at the market for $45 (the wood cost me about 2 cents per piece in petrol to get to the river mouth and back). The electricity, sandpaper, and clear finish added up to $2 worth at most. The rest was my time, doing it for pleasure rather than profit. The beauty was that I did make a profit from this simple piece.

From that one trip to the river, I sold pieces totalling over $400. I love driftwood. It is free and easy to find if you live anywhere near water. I remain particularly uncomfortable with the thought of purchasing wood when so much is available if you give yourself the time to search. I believe wholeheartedly in recycling as much wood as possible in this environment of ever-dwindling resources.

The next piece I considered was the curved base of a small tree. At first, I thought of a stingray as I was inspired by the curved portion of the wood. I had once seen a sculpture of a Manta Ray in the house of Diane Cilento, and I had longed thereafter to carve one myself. However, the stingray was not to be born from this particular piece of driftwood. The wood spoke to me in my dreams, telling me exactly what it wanted to be. Never have I had a clearer vision of a carving. The only thing that did not occur to me immediately was the base from which the animal would arise.

Cobra is born

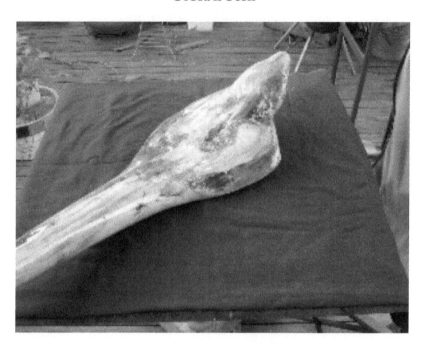

The outside of the curvature became the underside of Cobra, the head followed quickly with marbles glued into drilled eye sockets and a double strand of wire from a candle holder was shaped and inserted into a mouth cavity.

I did not chronicle the early stages of Cobra with pictures as I was lost in creativity to the exclusion of all else. An idea for a base eluded me for some time as I thought about appropriate fixtures. I considered a wood carved basket or coiled body until I finally stumbled across the idea of using another of the heavy logs I had lugged home. I decided I wanted a bit of the inside showing while keeping as much of the grey area intact. Driftwood is hard on machinery with sand and grit hiding in all the crevices. It pays to clean it with a pressure washer before you start. It can also be extra hard due to being 'pickled' by seawater. My little chainsaw struggled to hack off a section of wood and the consequent carving of the hole to mount the standing Cobra.

The beautiful grain and colours emerging from both pieces knocked me out. Cobra had a striking grain but was very soft and pulpy in sections. I would have to fortify the wood with a hardening agent or soak the wood in the clear urethane with which I would finish the piece. I chose the latter. The urethane hardened the wood nicely while giving it a lovely glossy finish. The piece of wood I cut off the base would actually go on to be another carving, Croc, which sold for $60 at auction. I was never truly happy with the base for Cobra, but it sold at an exhibition for $250. The man who purchased him was over the moon about finding such a gift for his reptile-loving son.

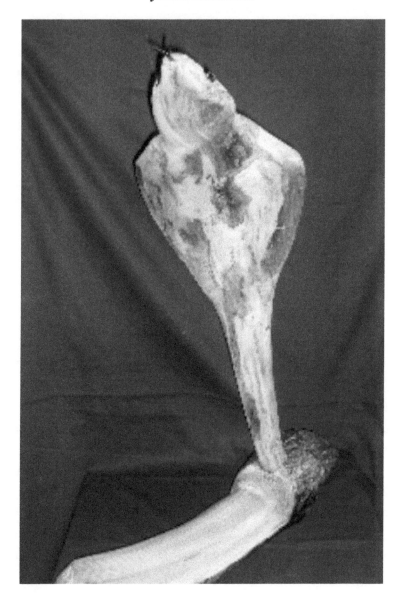

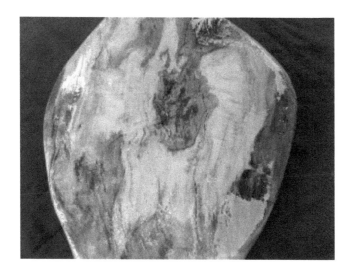

Croc started out as a carving seated in a rough block stand painted black. I changed that to a black backing board, to which I attached picture wire and 'D' rings to hang him on the wall. I did not do much with, Croc. He was shaped a little with stumpy legs and a few ridges on the tail, after which, he was sanded smooth, oiled and waxed. The barest outline of a crocodile was all that was required to make the shape immediately recognisable. The beauty in this piece came solely from the magnificent grain appearing just under the grey bark surface. Croc also had a couple of undulations not evident in the first picture that greatly increased his appeal.

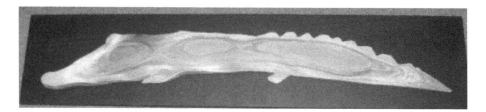

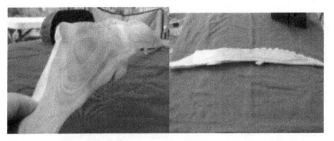

As you might imagine, not everything I create is sold or for sale. I have made whimsical yard art utilising driftwood. This hangs on my fence. I have made quirky reptile puppets that I have given away and I still have a driftwood pile from that day by the Yarra. The possibilities are endless if you have a little bit of imagination, a fair share of creativity, and most important of all, a partner to encourage and support you. Sandy, being an artist herself, could not hide her surprise when I began to create all the pieces I have shown so far, but her biggest surprise came when I tackled a quite complicated carving which I showcase later.

Spike arrived with a cheeky little dragon grin, springing from a piece of driftwood that most people wouldn't look at twice. I carved an eye, wire brushed him, then gave him a coat of oil and a 'D' ring hanger, total time: 15 minutes. He sold for $45 at a night market.

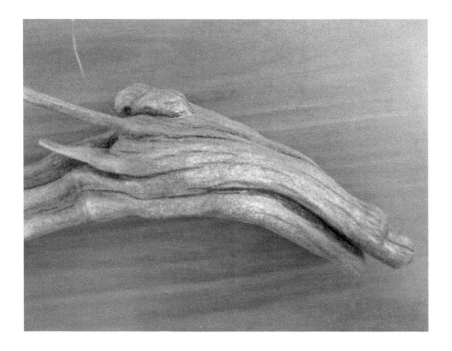

3 Styles

In my next carving, I wanted to capture the 'cute' factor. I found a large round crosscut slab of Oak. At least I think it was Oak. I am by no means an expert at identifying a species solely from its grain or colour. The trouble with a crosscut section is the splitting factor and the difficulty in attaining a smooth surface when going against the grain. Details in carvings can also be difficult to maintain with a crosscut section. When I looked closely at the round of wood sitting on its edge, the natural circumference reminded me of a baby bear's back. In particular, it reminded me of a photo I once saw, of Knut, the Berlin Polar Bear that gained notoriety around the world as one of the first Polar Bears born in captivity. In the photo I found on the internet, Knut is half sitting on the ice looking lost and frightened. This was the exact image and emotion I wanted to capture.

Mewling Bear

Starting with a round like this is a good head start with a carving as you are able to draw a rough outline with relative ease on the flat surface. With the guidelines drawn, I quickly went to work with the chainsaw, roughing out my piece. I started by cutting away the excess under the head – a bit like cutting away a section of pie. I had de-barked the wood to ensure that I knew how much material I had with which to work. It does not require fully seasoned wood to begin carving. It is often better to carve it green, as it is much softer to work with. You must, however, prepare for the inevitable cracking to appear as you carve.

There are ways to limit the severest cracking as the wood dries out. Placing a plastic bag over the carving will help to keep in the moisture. Storing the carving in a cool dry place when not working on it will also assist. In the previous picture, you can clearly identify the cracks appearing near the centre on the first day of carving.

I made a slip with the chainsaw while I was roughing out the snout, producing an unwanted cut beneath. It was too deep to disregard. I knew I could not simply sand the cut away so I decided to emphasise it, creating an open mouth. Mewling Bear was born. In the picture I was following, the mouth is closed. I surrendered once more to the will of the wood or perhaps just making up for my error? I found the hardest part of this carving was the correct shaping and placement of the ears. The *best* part of this particular piece was the lovely arched back. Everyone was drawn to pet the bear, even at these early stages of the carving.

Day 2 saw me shaping with the rasp and 4' angle grinder, a recent purchase, to assist me with the laborious task of removing large quantities of wood. Shaping the cavity between the four legs proved to be a very difficult task. I did not have a vice or a carving stand, so the wood needed to be placed on a table or on the ground in order to cut it with the chainsaw. Holding the wood with your feet while chainsawing features into it, is not safe, and scarcely conducive to accuracy. Trying to saw out a narrow gap is even harder. I ended up using chisels mainly. I now have a Power File that would have made easy work of it, but back then, I had to proceed the hard way. Sanding the tight areas in and around those spaces would prove the hardest yet.

With shaping completed, it was time to put my talent to the test by drawing in the nose, eyes, and ear holes. I used a knife to whittle those features into the face. In the picture I was following, his eyes appeared almond shaped and entirely flat. This is a two-dimensional trick when viewing pictures. My partner kindly reminded me that all eyes are spherical. A lens must have a curvature to provide sight, so I tried to make them as round as I could manage. By this time, I could have used a rotary tool with a flexible shaft to speed it all up. In hindsight, I am glad I did not have this tool because it forced me to learn some rudimentary knife techniques. Remember, I said I learned largely through my own research? Well, every time I came across a problem I could not solve myself, I went to the internet to determine a solution. The result was, that I spent a lot of time surfing the web.

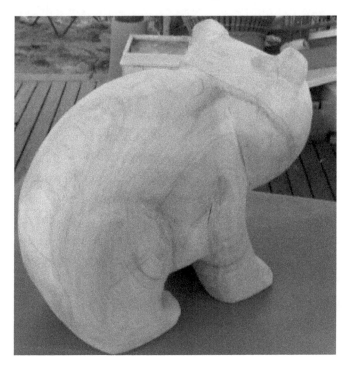

Everyone that laid eyes on Mewling Bear went, "Aw..." and immediately went to pat his shiny back. Mewling Bear was my first sale through an exhibition, selling half an hour after the doors opened. According to the organisers, he received a lot of attention.

I was contacted a week after the exhibition by a gentleman who told me that he and his wife had fallen in love with, Mewling Bear, but were too late to purchase him. He went on to say that while they were at the exhibition they saw a child actually giving the bear a kiss. I was thrilled that there had been such an emotional and tactile response to my carving. He asked me if I could carve them another Mewling Bear. I told him that I could not carve the *same* bear as all my pieces were one-off originals, however, I could carve something similar from different timber. I was paid a deposit and set about producing a second version of Mewling Bear.

I went out to my woodpile to find a likely log. I had no suitable size rounds like the original, so I had to find something that would accommodate the size and shape I required. Working on a commission places you in a peculiar headspace.

The emphasis is wholly on *you* to provide the agreed-upon item. It is not possible to let your imagination run wild because the form chosen takes precedence, adherence to that form is expected. The wood could say what it wanted, but unless it fell within the parameters of the commission, I could not bend to its will. As it turned out, I chose wisely, picking a log that suited my purposes without undue confrontation.

After debarking, I began with a rough drawing on two faces of the log. I must emphasise again that a crude drawing will suffice. It is important to utilise two sides if possible, to more clearly appreciate the proportions in a three-dimensional aspect. Once you are satisfied with the proportions, then sawing can proceed without too much guesswork involved. If you look closely at the first picture, you will notice a 'V' drawn at the top just behind the head? Every carving needs a starting place, one where you know there is little risk of destroying all the work done so far. A perfectly easy little section that will immediately give a good reference point to all the other cuts required thereafter. This time, I gave myself a little more space between the four legs.

Once the 'V' appears, carving can continue on the back region with a good idea of how deep to penetrate. I also marked the waste material between the legs with crosses for easier recognition while wearing safety goggles. After the back, the space in between the legs is the next area to work on. I wanted to try leaving the head as a block for now, as, Mewling Bear's, head had proven problematic. Getting the ears right in conjunction with the snout and eyes required more deliberation than I originally allowed. I knew this bear would end up being a little smaller than the first and I was happy with this. I was looking for as many points of difference as possible between this bear and the first.

I was already satisfied with the way the back was shaping up. That particular part of the carving could make or break the entire concept. I had to capture the 'cuteness' I managed to achieve with bear number one. This was not easy as I was essentially trying to reproduce an ambiance in a carving without copying the original.

Blocking out the head was next on the agenda. I was cautious with every stage of this carving, constantly referring back to my drawings and notes. I documented each step along the way in photographs just in case I needed reference material later on.

One thing I also do as I am carving, especially between carving days, is to view the photos I have taken. Looking at them on your computer screen gives them clarity. Another perspective is essential to artwork of any genre. Viewing your piece in a mirror may provide another perspective and is easily performed at any stage. Using the macro option on a digital camera will assist greatly for viewing close-up detail, picking up every imperfection, flaw, and mistake. If you are getting on a bit like me, it is important to wear your spectacles for close-up work. I use the cheap $2 magnifiers for carving purposes rather than risk damaging my expensive prescription glasses.

Do not fret over the rough appearance of your carving at this stage. As long as the proportions are acceptable, the rest is cosmetic and will receive attention later. Using a chainsaw to block out a carving of this size can leave the carver disillusioned at times, but practice will provide the carver with the confidence to persist.

Gaining expertise in anything at all requires time and patience. The only way to learn from mistakes is to make them. As hackneyed as that sounds, if you do not make many mistakes, you will learn nothing, gain nothing because you are taking no risks. I am constantly trying to challenge myself, egging myself on to attempt what I thought too difficult. There is no greater reward than achieving success when attempting an improbable task.

I did not believe I could carve until I gave it a go. I discovered a hidden talent and a dormant passion that exploded into my life with an enormous bang. I could say that I do not understand why it has taken me this long to discover woodcarving but in truth, I am acutely aware of the reasons. It has taken years to get past all the negativity heaped upon me throughout my life. I had to discard all that dross that impeded any progress in me for so long. A loving, supportive partner helps no end, but essentially, it is up to the individual to purge themselves. Stepping outside the circle requires courage and risk, but is well worth the effort. Without risk, there is only the mundane, predictable existence we sometimes build for ourselves. At the approach of fifty, I decided that an existence of total safety was not the path I sought, though, I no longer had the ambitions of fame and fortune so desirable to me in my youth. I now see those two imposters as nothing more than plastic baubles on a Christmas tree. I knew I had to break out of the funk that enveloped me earlier in life, to reach a potential I knew I could achieve.

Confidence is the key to all ventures worth taking. Confidence to rise to the occasion, to take the slings and arrows that may come your way. We live a finite length of time on this planet and it is far too short to toss away on *coulda*, *shoulda*, and *woulda*. To Hell with what anyone says about your art. If you are truly enjoying the experience it doesn't matter what others think. Fill up your *own* house with your creations if no one purchases them. Get a large property that you can turn into a natural gallery for your very own pleasure. If you find you cannot become as good as you would like to be in your genre, try a workshop or two. Find a mentor/tutor you are comfortable with and enlist their counsel in achieving your dreams. Mine came true, so can yours.

The time had come in the carving for shaping with my power grinder equipped with a sanding disc. I use a 16 grit sanding disc initially to wear away all the rough ridges left by the chainsaw. I used power tools extensively with this carving to cut down on time as much as possible. Remember, my time is now on the money clock. I quoted the same price as Mewling Bear which sold for $350 at the exhibition. I like to base my hourly rate at $20 at the very least, so time becomes a vital consideration when working on a commission.

The grain of the Yellow Birch is starting to show through even at this early stage of the carving. I use chisels and mallet to remove excess wood from the small areas in between the legs. One paw has developed an unforeseen arch. All you can do with such things is to go with the flow. Go as far as you are able, sand back the extremities of the hollow to even up the surface. Do not panic if the hollow is more than you bargained for. As long as the carving stands straight with all paws/feet on the ground, then all is well. Most imperfections are concealable in various ways, so never think that all is lost...for the most part. Final shaping, detailing of eyes, claws, mouth and sanding would take the most of day two on the project. Total time taken for, Lost Bear, came in at around ten hours. Total cost of finishing materials, electricity, chainsaw fuel, bar oil, and sanding sheets came to approximately $10. I did not become rich from the commission, but neither had I paid someone to take my art.

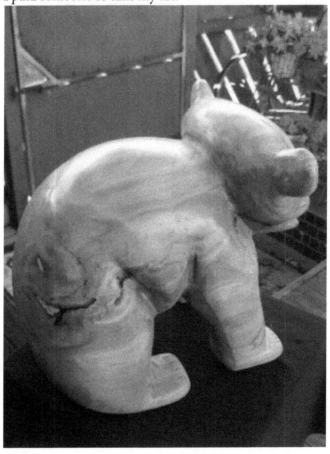

When my buyer arrived to take possession of, Lost Bear, he almost had the money out of his wallet before he entered the yard. I told him I would not take anything from him until he had thoroughly examined his sculpture. He only took a cursory glance at the bear before stating that he was entirely satisfied. He was so eager to hold the bear he could not wait. I received a Christmas card that year that read as follows; "Merry Christmas, Just a note to let you know I am still getting a kiss and a cuddle each day. Lost Bear, xx." It brought a lump to my throat I can tell you. What an unbelievably kind act from a happy customer who purchased one of my carvings. Who needs riches when you receive treasures such as that? I had been carving less than a year at that time.

4 Ambitions

As I browse through the photos on my computer to sort through the various carvings I might include in this book, I am surprised at the prolific rate at which I managed to produce carvings in such a short time. I do, however, now recall, that I was unemployed for some months when I first began. I hope to add two more volumes to this body of work eventually.

I simply must include two more projects in *this* volume, though. The first one I will share with you was by far my most ambitious to date. There were several stages during the creation when I believed I had erred beyond redemption. I persevered, as do I with 99% of my pieces, to complete the carving. When I first explained the concept to my partner, who has a vivid imagination, seeing the most unusual things in everyday items, she was quite doubtful, to say the least.

Unfortunately, I didn't take a picture of the log before I began hacking away with the chainsaw. Imagine if you will, a cylindrical block with two lumpy protrusions. One protrusion at the top of the block extended toward the 'front', while the second appeared lower and to the right when viewing the log front on. The unlikely subjects I saw in the wood were a couple of heads peering out and two bodies competing with one another for a better vantage point. I wonder if you recognise the piece already. I do not imagine it will take you long. The unlikely subjects chosen for this carving do not rate highly on most people's likeability scale, but nothing could deter my purpose.

I had no drawings of a *pair* of subjects in the corresponding positions for reference, only some individual subjects reproduced from the internet. There is no possible way I could ever hope to get a picture of the exact scene I had in mind for this carving. It was very slow going as I stood back many times to gain perspective, to gauge the depths, and proportions of the two subjects. I cannot ever adequately explain how I saw this carving so clearly, nor do I have such clear visions for every carving I attempt. This is one log that spoke to me loud and clear without reservation.

One thing I have not shared about carving with a chainsaw that requires mention is the advent of muscle shock. Anyone using a petrol chainsaw will relate to the condition caused by the vibrations delivered by a petrol chainsaw, or any other power tool with heavy vibrations. It is very important to take it in stages, resting for periods when using such tools extensively. I am always one to attack a project with gusto, forgetting all else in my wake. I learned early on to take my rest breaks or else my poor old body would feel it dearly the following day. Indeed, there were days I could barely lift my arms when I disregarded my own advice. Severe muscle shock can be very painful for several days afterward.

I have just about roughed out my slimy friends, but one crucial task remains for which I must be thoroughly prepared. The two bodies remain attached to one another like Siamese twins. I need to make one vital chainsaw cut to separate them. It is super critical to ensure the cut is deadly accurate or the project will fall far short of the mark. I delay the moment interminably as I study the carving from every angle, to discern the correct angle the tip of the chainsaw must take, in order to penetrate the exact place to make the carving possible.

I breathed a huge sigh of relief when I successfully separated the pair. I cannot emphasise enough the importance of ensuring the success of that one cut. Again, one cut can make or break a piece. The rough-out proceeded nicely, though, I did come across a void in the mouth/beak area of the lower animal. Once the crucial moment had passed, it was time to start shaping with the angle grinder and rasp, still my favourite part of any carving.

You will undoubtedly recognise, Dancing Morays, from the book cover by this stage. The shaping proceeds surprisingly well under my careful ministrations. The two eels look splendidly slippery and slimy. I laboured long and hard to ensure I followed the curvature of the body accurately, determined to get the underside fin as realistic as possible. I did this for some hours, feeling quite proud of myself until I studied the computer-generated picture again that night.

I did not have the subject's picture at hand while I was carving because of a temporary glitch with the printer, which proved to be my downfall. It exemplified the reason I say to keep a picture handy at **ALL** times throughout the carving. All the trouble I went to ensuring the bottom fin mirrored the body with a few separate undulations to show movement, were to no avail. Moray Eels have no bottom fin and I have no idea what gave me that impression! Hours of hard labour to produce a feature that does not belong! My heart sank when I realised the extent of my mistake. The problem with making mistakes when carving in wood are whether or not they are redeemable. It is quite possible that in many cases there is insufficient wood to remedy the error. Fortunately for me, that was not the case. It was the opposite. It would only mean removing a mountain of work.

My next conundrum came about as I viewed the photos on my computer screen. The carving appeared to be missing an aspect I had not considered. I was happy with the two twisting bodies and I had a plan for the base, but the carving appeared bare. It needed an addition of sorts, something bordering on a habitat to place the eels in an environment.

Around the time I was carving the Morays, the local council began an operation to clean up the trees on the footpaths around our area. These trees were either hindering power lines or rotten and diseased. I ran after them with my barrow collecting heaps of logs from a great variety of different trees. One of my rescued logs had a marvellous leaf-like shape to the cross-section. It was Coastal Tea-tree in a beautiful red/pink colour. I thought it might look a little like coral if I carefully placed it within the carving. I cut a slab off the log and smoothed it with a grinder.

I found the Tea Tree to be a very hard wood which meant it would shine up like polished agate once finished. With wood, the more densely the fibres are packed together, the harder the wood and the better it takes to perfect smooth finishes. Cleaning the bark and dirt from between the myriad of rifts and valleys took forever. I then made a cradle to seat the 'coral', securing it with glue and dowel. I had not yet oiled or waxed the coral. I had sanded much of the Morays, although getting in between the bodies was proving to be a challenge.

I don't know if you have ever seen footage or stills of a moray eel? If so, you will know that there can never be a 'correct' shape to perfect. These morphing creatures tend to take on many shapes and twists in their general movement. My partner's son commented that the top eel's head was far too large. I begged to differ once I had thoroughly checked over every picture I could find of Morays. It pays never to listen to critics or detractors, especially in the middle of a carving. I never listen to anyone anymore. I am either right or wrong, but in the end, it is my reputation on the line and a piece will either sell or not.

Near the end of the sanding process, I found a piece of driftwood that I know I could never find again in a million years of searching. I seriously doubt I could ever have found a more suitable prop to compliment my diorama. It was the final missing piece for this carving. It gave the two Morays a purpose for twisting about in the fashion I had carved them. It fitted the exact shape of the two bodies without a single modification.

It was nearing Easter while I was carving this piece. Some friends asked if we would puppy-sit for them in the country. It was difficult for me to choose between wanting to continue with my carving and my desire for a spell in the mountains. I finally decided to take my gear with me to continue the carving while we cared for their newborn pups, chooks, ducks, vegetables and flowers. I managed to pick up a decent limb or two of Blackwood and Walnut while in the mountains.

I finished the sanding and had a go at painting, much to my distaste. The base was painted with a gouache of greens, blacks, and ochres. I could not have asked for a nicer couple of days up in that fresh air with a superb mountain scene as a backdrop. I found it very hard to cope with all that natural stimulation, carving, and a beer or two as well!

By the time we headed home I had the Morays oiled and waxed, so all I had to do was affix the extraneous parts to finish the piece. I had carved in the eyes with a pinprick of black paint in the centres. The grain in the yellow Birch was outstanding once again.

I look at this piece a year onwards and marvel at my audacity to attempt such an ambitious piece so early in my carving experience. My partner had some serious doubts about my vision for that block of wood when I first announced the presence of two heads. I found it amazing that I could follow that vision through to completion. A pair of eels may not be the subject of great appeal, but the wood spoke to me in a clear voice, revealing its desire for that log. I humbly followed and completed a very satisfying journey into a carving of which I am most proud.

5 Rewards

I lied! I still have two more projects to share with you. The first is a project that anyone thinking of carving as a hobby could easily attempt. I am not talking about the subject, only the process. I said I couldn't draw and I hold strongly to that premise. I also said that you do not have to be good at drawing to proceed in this art form. One of the easiest methods of producing the desired shape from wood is to find a picture of the subject you wish to carve, print it out in the exact size you require, and then simply cut out the shape.

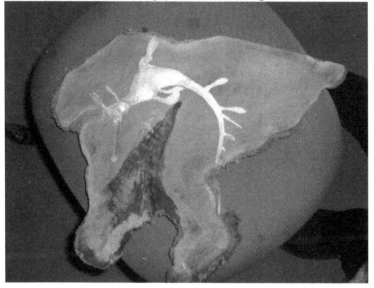

Lay the cut-out onto the slab of wood you have decided upon, in the position you desire. Trace around the outside of the cut-out with a highly visible dark pencil. Using whatever you have at hand, a jigsaw, a bandsaw, or a coping saw, cut out the figure you have drawn. Be more careful than I am when choosing your subject. Too many small extraneous appendages are difficult to cut around and nearly impossible to keep attached. I lost several during the cutting out process on this little Weedy Sea Dragon. I also recommend you use a softer wood than the Tea tree I have used for this piece. Once you have cut out the object, you will have to begin rounding, shaping and generally cleaning up between fins etc. If you are using soft wood, then a utility knife or a *sharp,* carving knife will come in handy for much of the shaping. There was no way a knife would have *looked*

at the hardwood I was using, so I went back to my perennial favourite, the wood rasp.

I was in the wars from the beginning with this little creature. First, the head plume broke off, then the neck plume, then several tail fins. I was close to despair, but I believed I could do it if I just persevered. Glue can do marvels, while wire and paint can do the rest. I started the shaping process on this one by attacking the snout first. If I couldn't get that right then there was no point in continuing. I had to make sure that the snout remained centred.

You will notice the distinct lack of 'bits' on this piece. Many 'bits' fell off during the various stages of this carving. I wonder then if you notice the ugly grey lump onto which I have decided to mount Weedy. It is an off-cut from Cobra. If anyone had told me that the fantastic colours and grain of Cobra would appear out of that implausible lump of wood, I would have chuckled heartily. You never can tell what is hiding under the grey exterior, especially true of driftwood. It was very pulpy wood, so I soaked it in a solution of diluted wood glue to harden it.

The pieces that had broken off Weedy were glued back on once I had shaped them to my satisfaction. I used thin wire to attach the plumes as I did not believe toothpick size wood to be strong enough to withstand the rigors of a handled carving. It is important to remember that carvings need moving and handling many times in their lives, even cleaning, and re-waxing. My partner made sure I got that message loud and clear as she nearly destroyed several of my pieces in her daily movements about the house. I am very happy that I continued with Weedy despite the hindrances. There are always setbacks to most ambitious projects, so treat them as challenges rather than failures and you will avoid the irritation every time something goes awry.

I really hope I have inspired someone to give carving a go after witnessing the ease involved in delivering an acceptable carving. Begin with an uncomplicated subject, download a good photograph and the rest is straightforward. By the way, the glue on the base does dry to a very clear finish. I was a little concerned as well when it took quite a long time to do so.

My last project that I want to share with you is a competition entry given a Viewer's Choice Award. Arts Blitz is a competition in which the entrants have twenty-four hours to produce a work of art relating to a theme announced at five o'clock on a Friday afternoon. The finished artwork is then required to be handed in at five pm the following day (Saturday).

The theme for Arts Blitz 2011 was 'Green'. I struggled with the theme for half an hour or more before deciding on a green tree frog. I quickly downloaded several pictures as reference guides and decided upon a log from which to carve the subject, high-tailed it to my factory and prepared to work all night with noisy equipment (and not upset the neighbours).

I worked diligently until 10 pm when disaster struck!

I took a very large chunk out of the frog's left leg as I was madly chiselling. Gluing the chunk back into place was not an option, even super-gluing it would not work, as I would not be able to chisel the piece afterward. I certainly could not hand the piece in without a left leg! I thought about cutting the head off, attaching it to a clear acrylic sheet as if the frog's head was emerging from the water. That did not work. It looked like I was serving up a frog's head on a clear dinner plate. I can tell you now, that I had pretty well given up. I was exhausted, dirty and very tired.

I sat there quite bereft at my failure, wondering what I would say to my partner who had also entered the competition. I had no other idea in my head. Nothing said 'Green' to me. I did bring another log with me just in case, but I had run out of steam mentally and physically. Five hours with a chainsaw after working for eight hours during the day and my body really began to feel the strain. I hated the thought of quitting, but I saw no alternative.

It was then I finally decided I'd had quite enough of my own bellyaching. It was time to put my theory to the test, to put into practice that which I had preached so loud and so often. Without a single thought in my head, I began to de-bark the backup log, quietly allowing the log to speak to me if it chose. For the first time in my life, I began a project without a clue as to the outcome.

I shuddered at the thought of beginning a new carving at that time of night, but the thought that I would not be handing in an artwork urged me onward. I was unsure if my experiment would work, but I was sure as heck going to do *something*.

A dimple in the wood appeared after I de-barked a section on the 'bottom' of the log. The log spoke softly, but the words were not yet clear. Something was materialising in my head but I almost dismissed it as weariness descended upon me. It was not until I had removed all the bark that the hint transformed itself into a solid idea. I knew then what I'd be carving for the 'Green' theme.

I needed a basic design as nothing too complex could be achieved in the remaining time. I could not work *all* night long, as it is extremely dangerous to work with power equipment when the senses are dull with tedium. My idea did not overly excite me and I had no reference material. I was very familiar with the subject, but a picture sitting next to me would have comforted me no end.

As I began to use the chainsaw the wood engaged me, guiding my thoughts and actions. I saw the shape emerging clearly as the hours melted away until one o'clock in the morning. It was only when I had reached the point that I knew I could make the timeline, that I began to relax, allowing fatigue to take hold. I had to get some sleep before I became a danger to myself.

I was immensely proud of myself for following my own convictions, for believing in the espoused rhetoric my dear partner and friends had endured from me. I would have something to hand in for one reason only - that I did not quit. I listened to the wood with an open heart and mind.

New York Granny

This was the state of the apple when I left at one o'clock on Saturday morning. I did not have the time or the confidence to take pictures earlier during the carving. I was running on pure adrenalin, which forbade me to stop until I knew I had the carving in hand. The apple needed sanding and the leaf at the top needed shaping, though I would not try to get the stem too thin as I feared further mishaps. I would not tempt fate.

I returned at four o'clock in the morning to continue, and although I had slept only three hours, I felt rested and rejuvenated. I broke into a sweat during the early hours of the cool morning. I laboured to produce the smoothness on the carving indicative of my style. I utilised every power tool I owned to cut down on the amount of time it would require to make this carving a unique work of art.

New York Granny did not win the 3D component of the competition, which did not upset me, though it did cause me to question the decision when viewing the other entries. I happened across one of the Arts Blitz judges a week later.

The judge explained that the panel did not believe my piece was produced in the twenty-four hour time period stipulated, thereby dismissing the entry. The judge even went on to say that a lack of smell added to their concern! I was astounded.

Vindication was mine after winning the Viewer's Choice Award, by a large majority. The event organiser placed my piece in the centre of the room, as he believed it to be an outstanding work of art. Everyone that saw the apple believed it should have won. For me, New York Granny had come out a winner anyway. I carve for the pure love of it and for the general public. I am not interested in impressing officious so-called artists and would not stand for the dismissal of my piece with my integrity brought into question. Winning the People's Choice was a far greater reward than the opinion of three judges.

I rose to a definite challenge offered to me by a competition and a mishap. It would define me as a person, as a believer in myself, as an artist, and as a woodcarver in particular. When I opened my soul to the wood, it whispered to me in soft undertones. In turn, I whispered back, embarking on my journey into woodcarving.

The End

Other Titles by Josef Peeters:

Giving Up:
A State of Mind

Not a self-help book. Not a hand-holding Kumbaya singing, good-feeling therapy attempt. Not an effort to give evidence of expertise in anything other than failure. It explores my way out of the mess in which I found myself. If it helps someone else find the state of mind necessary to do the same; fan-frigging-tastic. If not; stiff!
See purchase links on Josef's Author website:
http://lakesidecaravanpark.wixsite.com/josef

Dumped

Nothing takes the fun out of a vacation faster than a plane crash. Except for a confession of infidelity just before the oxygen masks drop. Read **DUMPED** to see who survives.

See purchase links on Josef's Author website:

http://lakesidecaravanpark.wixsite.com/josef

ABOUT THE AUTHOR

Josef lives with his partner, Sandy, in Moulamein NSW, where they own and manage a caravan park. He has been an actor on stage and screen, author of poetry, play scripts, an autobiography, and now, as a woodcarver, he embarks on what he hopes will become
a three part series of woodcarving journals.
See Josef's creations from this booklet and many others
on his website:
http://carverjoe.weebly.com

Lightning Source UK Ltd.
Milton Keynes UK
UKHW010937060223
416537UK00002B/452